Where I Arrived

Where I Arrived

A Journey of Love in It's Many Forms

By Takayla P. "TK" Carlton

To the queer community

To believers of Christ

To believers of Christ
who are also queer

To women

To Black women

To those who have loved

To those who have not
been loved in return

To those who still search for love

I first want to give an honor and praise to God

Thank you to my village who continues to love,
accept, and support all that I am and do

Thank you to the attentive readers of this book in manuscript form:
Mike Bonifer, Sarah McHale, and Janis Albuquerque

Thank you to Mama's Kitchen Press for handling this work with such care

Thank you to The Community Literature Initiative

Thank you to all those who have ventured on the journey
of reading this book

Contents

Venture Two: Journeying to Love

Chapter Three: The Book of Love

Chapter 5: The Book of Self

Audio Recordings

Artwork and Photographs

Preface

I didn't have the privilege of embracing vulnerability and living in
my truth as a young, Black, queer, Baptist girl in white America.
I was taught to conceal my true self, fearing rejection and harm.
Yet, guided by God's protective hand, I've embarked on a journey
towards authenticity. Now, I navigate life from a place of love,
rather than fear.

This book is a journey to discover such love, embodying
the duality of both the secular and the sacred. It is a testament
to God's purpose working through me, born from
my human experiences, spiritual revelations, and love.
May it offer you solace, may it provoke introspection,
may it allow you to feel seen, may it fulfill its divine purpose
within you.

Venture One

Journeying Through Limerence Longings and The Letting Go

Chapter One

The Book of Limerence

Emancipated

Security is tapping on the door

Her hands
My thighs
Cornsilk yellow fluorescents flickering
Mirrors opaque from tha steam we are brewing
Tightly enclosed within flint gray walls clothed in carvings
of numbers promising a good time
Scents of cheap perfume and lust linger
I am here
Bathing in her bourbon butterscotch kisses
Tonguing her soliloquies in the mazes of me
Something wise about the story she's telling
Something church about it

Security is knocking on the door

"This stall is occupied! Damn!"

Verboten actions are taking place
in the first floor women's restroom
On Juneteenth
Abstinence was my allegiance just a few moments ago
A soldier
An obligation to his word
To this temple

But isn't it my duty
to liberate this black body presented in front of me?
On this day of all days
Shouldn't I
Embrace a Black woman
Hold her so tight that her ancestors feel it
So that her mamaw finally gets tha affection and
recognition she deserves
Let me bleed for this Black woman
Let me bleed how Christ did on that cross
Crucify me so that I may be loved
So that I may be worshiped for once
On this day
The nineteenth of June
Let my flesh be emancipated and I bear the
consequences when the
scrub-jay sings

Security is banging on the door

And I choose to ignore
I'm tryna be her dinner until I become her breakfast
Seep my syrup sticky into her palms
She is stirring into me
like hot bisque in my blood
Bouillon bones
My syllables boiling up her throat
Her gums fill with my name
I pervade her

Security is shaking the damn door

Candied promises murmured in my ear are no more
Drunken hands reluctantly accept the tedious task of twisting
my shirt back to its proper state
One nipple ring lost
and the other jealous of how it was misplaced
I open the door and irony slaps us both in the face
A man
Bereft of seasoning
stands before us

We brazenly walk past with shackled hands, segregated lips,
and unsatisfied bellies

We Are

Not

Free Here

In the Shadows of Unreturned Love

I think of you the way you think of him

Highly

And in between each breath that I take

Another Tuesday Thought

I want so badly to remember what your lips
taste like

So that I may understand why
I can't forget how they made me feel

Unicorn

For PaladinLost9 from Reddit

My chest beats backwards in your sight
My lips are tired of longing for you
My phone never received your "good night"
Grieves the absence of your "good mornings" too

If I were a poet, my sonnets would share stories of one
more soulmate in addition to two
If I were a siren, each note would bend to your whispers
as harmonic tone
If I were a sorceress, I'd erase our thwarting circumstances
with a simple brew
If I were *Homo sapien*, I'd rise from dust and become
bone of your bone

My mind overflows with your names
My fingers clasps together in prayer
whispering for release from your chains
My understanding of love blurs in the temptation of
your snare

Only tucked between your sheets, I am worthy of your
consideration
Folded within unpromising futures, yet I love you both
without hesitation

Fever

When you fell ill
I put Vicks VapoRub under your nose and on your chest

When your voice grew hoarse
I hummed you a prayer over hot tea and honey

When your fever became stubborn
I sat a cold rag on your forehead and
cooked bone broth soup with turmeric from scratch

One onion
One celery stalk
Two sticks of carrots
Two shakes of black pepper
A pinch of salt
And a whole heap of love

When I was not myself
you looked at me and said   goodbye

Situationship

It isn't easy loving you like this, you know?

It isn't

what grandmother would call lady-like

what the pastor would call proper

what the doctor would call healthy

what the elders declare wise

It isn't easy loving you like this, you know?

With all of me and half of you

When you look at me

I forget that your eyes are not rivers of Proverbs

streaming divine truth

but merely eyes that lust

I forget that your hands are not safe havens for

heart that cradles and croons

but merely hands that touch

I forget that your lips are not citadels of mud and brick,
ensuring the safety of a home
but merely lips that manipulate with kiss

When I am with you, I forget that you do not ask me on dates
or brag about me to your friends
I forget that I am your secret
your night thing

It is only when you leave that I remember your
absence

Unclaimed Heart

Though you are not mine
My loving belongs to you

This can't be healthy

For the Possibility of Love

Don't be a damn fool
You are desired only
When you yearn worship

Sleeping Through Declarations

I want nothing but to love you

You lay here, heavy and gentle
I listen to the musical whispers of wind,
I call snoring and you call nonexistent,
escaping from your lungs
I don't mind indulging you in this joke
Much as I don't mind the weight of your presence
compressing me deeper into your ethereal whole
with each breath that you take

You lay here, heavy and gentle
restful as the moon itself
I am ocean
forever pulled in by the gravitational force of you
The bending of waves write my heart's confessions
in the sand below your light
In the quiet of night your breath song shushes such
love letters
It is here where I am made to hide my love
To withhold my giving
in efforts to not disturb the peace you've found
through the dreams of your slumber

Heavy and gentle, you lie here
I press prayers in the form of kisses
into the flesh of you
speaking your wildest dreams into existence
You turn toward me
eyelids remaining shut
and extend your reach
I am held hallow
I scan your being for answers I cannot find
You must feel the disturbance in my tide
because suddenly I am no longer in your arms

It is here I am reminded that I am ocean
Passionate and wild
I crash waves of unyielding yearning
I set seaside declarations afire
Currents aflame
led by the pull of you
fierce and untamed
I could storm lightning sparks of desire into
the depths of your soul

If only you'd open your eyes
and let me

You are not yet ready to receive the gulf of love
I desperately long to shore
beyond the trough of possibility
beyond the series of sensations found behind the
resting of eyelids
Yet, under the trance of your sleeping symphony
the torching of sand-written love letters has become
nighttime ritual
Burning for your heart's S.O.S. rescue

I say all this to say

I could love you
if only you'd open your eyes
And let me

Unattainable Soulmates

As the fine hairs on your skin keep me warm
and the soft hush of your prayerful eyes
lull me into green pastures

I think of God

Of how I see him through you

And what he must think of us
lying here
loving one another

secretly

How Come You Don't Call Me?

I call you
No answer
I check your location
You are out again with a friend
And
I am here
Wrapped up all within myself
By myself
You are probably on your fourth shot by now
Drowning in your drunken thoughts
On the edge of giving into their temptations

I am here
Strings stretched across my chest
Bending with each tug as you pedal through
Coloring each moment with soul melodies
Tapping your feet to the harmony of my
Longing for you

I am left wondering
"Will you ever choose me?"
And
"Why do I stay in places where I am not chosen?"

I am here
Singing the blues to your name
We were strung together to compose this ballad
Made for each other
But
I am here
Wrapped up all within myself
By myself

And you are out singing to another tune

House

When I was ten, I remember playing house
I remember a thousand onyx strands, shiny and swinging at the waist
of the neighbor's niece
I remember leaning in to kiss her
I am mom and she is mom and we hold hands and eat ice cream for lunch
and drink red Kool-Aid from Hello Kitty mugs

I remember the scold screaming from my brother's eyes
as he softly read the Google search "two girls kissing"

I pretend to like boys for twelve years after that day

It is late afternoon in spring
Against velvet of an emerald couch, my back softens
I daydream of us
as I cut the ends of knotless braids
careful not to trim the hair beneath
Long, patterned, plaited ropes that you found pleasure in
tugging nights before
now lie in a plastic bag to the left of me
The television slowly fades to mute
A brush of whispers caress my ear
professing me "beautiful"
declaring me "baby"
I can feel again your hands reaching for my breast,
pressing firmly at my heart

I pretend that I am yours
I pretend that you love me

It is well after sunset
I crawl into bonnet,
sinking into bed, when I think of you
My sheets turn stage
your memory a songstress
as your scent sings stories of our time together

You see,
you left days ago but
you forgot your daydreams at my doorstep
your fingerprints smudged on my heart
your singing scent humming between my sheets

When I was twenty-four I had a crush on a woman
I remember leaning in to kiss her
I pretend I am mom and she is mom
and she is unafraid to love me before sunset and we
hold hands at red-carpet events and stain champagne
glasses with red lipstick

I pretend she holds me and means it

I pretend that I am ten again
and no longer have to play make believe   to be loved

Undisciplined Devotion

When you gather my giving
all I ask in return is that you call my
undisciplined loving
beautiful
which others pronounce foolish

Journal Prompts for Limerence Longings

1. Who is someone I need to stop being delusional about? How am I delusional about them? How are they hindering me/holding me hostage?

2. What fake scenarios have I created in my head that I often replay? Do I want these scenarios to become a reality? Why are the scenarios so prominent in my mind?

3. In what romantic situations or relationships do I need clarity? What can I do to gain this clarity, even if the other party isn't capable of giving it?

4. Are there other potential sources of connection or fulfillment in my life that I've been neglecting?

5. How can I cultivate a sense of gratitude and appreciation for the relationships and experiences that bring me joy?

Affirmations for Limerence Longings

1. I release attachment to outcomes and trust in the divine timing of love in my life

2. I am resilient and capable of healing

3. I am loved abundantly, with or without them

4. I deserve to be with someone who values and reciprocates my love

5. I deserve romance

6. I deserve vulnerability

7. I deserve clear communication

8. I deserve a safe space to grow

9. I deserve a love that chooses to love me

10. I honor my feelings with kindness and understanding, knowing that they are valid and worthy of acknowledgment

Chapter Two

The Book of Letting Go

“At this point it's not grace, it's sacrifice”

God, Why Did You Allow Me Someone That I Could Not keep?

Maybe I needed to experience your spirit to experience
more of myself

Maybe I needed to feel your touch to feel freedom anew

Maybe I needed to know your heart to know of love
poems and growing pains too

Maybe I needed to fall in love with you to fall out of love
with attachment

A Journey Through the Thorns

It is ironic that you brag on how you love abidingly,
yet you could not find eternity with me

Loving you is like a barefooted journey through an
endless garden, each step revealing new layers of beauty
and thorns snagging at my heels

No matter how many times I suffix
my feelings for you with an "ed,"
they are still in present tense

It is ironic that you brag on how you love fiercely,
yet you could not find any fire for me

Loving you is like shielding a flame from the wind,
wary of if it is better to protect this warmth or un-cup
my hands allowing the glow to spread
to burn
through gusts of truth

I am reluctant to tell you
who you really are in an effort to spare your feelings
I'm not sure if this is cowardly or considerate

It is ironic that you take pride in exuding settling love,
yet you never consider how your actions torment me

Loving you is like rowing a tranquil river, unaware of the
turbulent rapids ahead

I am exhausted from loving you
through your uncertainty,
so let me help you make up your mind

If you find it hard to hold me in the light of day,
please love me enough to let me go

If I am worthy of your deep conversations, your flirtatious eyes,
your sexual intimacy, but not your consideration of building
a romantic relationship with,
then love me enough to let me go

If you notice that I am staring into those christening eyes
of yours in search of heaven, knowing that you can only
provide me with earthly things,
please love me enough to let me go

I was prepared to love you past the bounds of time,
through burning citadels,
standing in the eye of a hurricane,
but you were too focused on my gender to see my heart
Yet, I still love you beyond your Venus's comprehension,
beyond the moon and the stars,
beyond the fear of sexual orientation

Isn't it ironic that I take pride in how much I love you,
yet I do not love myself enough to
Let
You
Go

Caution: Safety Goggles Required When Handling Heterosexual Experimental Phases

I once fell in love with a straight woman

A Heterosexual's hypothesis
Experimental expectations
Exploding my senses
Surpassing self
Surpassing self-saturation

I loved her in ways society says I shouldn't
Naturally, unnatural

Secret seductions—sourcing serotonin snuggles
Torrid testimonials
Riveting romances, reassuring
affairs
Intrusive inquisitive impulses
Gay gazes
Helium highs holding honesty hostage
Test tube tales

I once fell in love with a straight woman

Her hips told stories of undeserving boys playing healer,
playing doctor,
causing chemical catastrophes
Her chest chanted chimes of concrete men
conquering her within

Christening eyes catalyzing chaos within me
Heated exhales entrapping everlasting hope
Highly held cheek bones hosting delusions, slipping
out of hand hemmed lips
spilling their way
inside
Beckoning beyond all sense of consequence

I be baking soda, she be vinegar
We quiet and explosive and controlled and messy
and fearful and unflinching
all at the same time
Beaker breaking erupting reactions
like enzyme

Her hands trailed my being like wild horses
on a spring Wyoming plain
Sensual and imprudent
Taking me across moss-veiled trails
Leading me to enchanted places where love and sin were
no longer synonymous
Crackling stems of pine-green vines wrap around us twice
pulling me in closer
Luminous petals of blue bird notes singing of desire
through the clouds
harmonizing with russet doe eyes
professing her love, long before her lips ever knew

That night, fear escaped my body like steam fleeing
heated arms on a crisp day
And returned when winter whispered that all of our
enchanted trail runs were just a trial run
And returned   again   in spring
when the caterpillars I placed in her belly
underwent a metamorphosis of sexual realization
and flew away
Her once cocooned uncertainty reduces me to
just a phase
The kind that my mother had hoped for me

I once fell in love with a straight woman
A Heterosexual's hypothesis

Her lips told stories of
taking but never giving
of wanting but never choosing
of lusting but never loving

Inconsiderate elbows flinging flasks of hazardous
kisses from men and present flirting with other
women
Stinging my eyes, eroding my love, piercing my soul

Next time I will not ignore the signs
I will wash my hands of previous relational filth,
wear steel-toe boots to prevent another
from stepping on my toes, put on a white coat that
shields my heart

Next time
I will wear
safety goggles

Indigo Confessions

Does yo momma know?

That her daughter sips champagne from my breast
like she would a slim, thin-stemmed glass

Does yo momma know?

That your nightly fantasies consist of you and I
between indigo cottoned sheets

Does yo momma know that I love you?

That you change my name from friend to baby
every time the sun sets and the door closes

Does yo momma know?

That you do not treat me as lover or friend but as
afterthought
as faucet
to be drained
to quench
to soothe
yielding to your caress

Does yo momma know?

That I loved you

Blanket

The day we were chosen to be only friends
And just that
I said prayers of strength
Prayers to be released from the shackles of
our fate
And held you only in the corridors of my mind
Blanketed my feelings and tucked away my affections

I will always love you

But you cannot be mine

So each night I sleep walk
Waltzing to the tune of your laughter
Every step echoing my deepest affections

I look forward to meeting you there,

In my dreams

Acceptance

The possibility of us was always greater than our reality

Holding On

Loving you is my favorite form of self-sabotage

Breadcrumbing

No one tells you how to get over a situationship
There are no talk show topics,
self-help books,
or motherly advice
to ease the loss of such love
A love found
between

the spaces
of convenience,
need,
and hope

No one tells you that the worst break-ups are from
the loves that don't break,
the loves that were
never really built in the first place,
the unrequited loves,
the loves that turn to obsession
and delusion,
as artificial fillers for the
between

until you are summoned again
to fulfill a need of theirs again

No one tells you that such love
is much like reading a book
then watching the movie
and realizing that your imagination
is far more creative
and kinder than any director's eye

No one tells you that they will always choose
the stale popcorn and two-hour film
over putting in effort to learn the book that is you

No one validates the heavy that follows a
situationship
because after all it was never really real
the intimacy,
the time spent,
the changing of names,
the sharing of body
was nothing more than a fever dream
fabricated in a realm of lies

There's something beautiful about the way it breaks
your heart
Something comforting
in the vanilla and caramel swirl ice-cream
that follows,
in the chafed bitterness from day old red wine
staining your tongue
Something exhaling
in the shit-talking and crooked smiles
from your homegirls, reassuring that
"you were too good for them anyhow,"
the kind of compliment given out of
obligation or pity rather than truth
Like Christians who give a tenth of their spoils
but do so grudgingly instead of cheerfully

And as a dog returns to its own vomit,
There's something foolish
in the rhythm of feet strutting back the second
they show interest
Something alluring
about the way it gives you hope
and then snatches it away
like a whip
lifting from black skin
eager to taste blood again

And though your homegirls advice is a testament
of love,
it doesn't really matter what they say
because no one ever taught them
how to grieve something given, but never really had
to begin with,
either

I Now Know What It Means When They Say That You Can't Love Someone [Properly] Until You Love Yourself

I see how they hurt you
I see what you've accepted
I see what you have called love
What I cannot see is how someone as heavenly as you
As ethereal
As wise
As enchanting
settles for the bare minimum

Because of this I cannot be angry with you
for not loving me how I deserve to be loved
Because I see how you have not yet learned how to
love yourself
And it is reflected in how you give love,
unsure
distant
afraid

I hope for you in ways I hope that you hope for yourself
I pray for you in ways I pray that you pray for yourself
I love you in ways you do not yet love yourself
Consequential
      to how you love me
          and why
      this love   isn't

enough

Hopeful Thinking

I always thought that if I left
you would realize how much you actually do
love me
and come back running with mascara laced down
your face
pink proteas in your left hand
and hope in your right

But like petals masking a rose's thorns,
expectations sting

Expectations

Haven't they shown you
how human they are with you?
People disappoint.

The Listener

You and I are a bittersweet ballad echoing
the forgotten lyrics of a love song

I think of you in flashes of nights when you'd rest
your weary head in the cavity of my chest and let
me love all of the blues outta you

We were like slow jazz
Each deep conversation a walking bass
keeping the rhythm of our breath
Bent note laughs
Legato longings
And Staccato stares
careful not to let anyone notice the song we were writing

You and I were like the intro to a '70s soul song
No words need to be said to know what was felt
Riding the beat to your lips in pure melodic magnificence
We were wild peaceful tones
like the symphony of cricket legs calling one another to unity

You and I are a harp's story
I, your beautifully-strung instrument
You, the sitting musician
Plucking my strings to melancholy melodies
Placing me down and picking me up at your convenience

And oh   how I longed to be strung by you
just
to be
touched by you

You and I are vocal runs in a eight-minute-long
gospel song
Continuous notes of rapid ups and downs
letting the spirit guide us
Grit knee and bloody scabbed prayers
pleading to feel the Holy Ghost in one another

just

one

last

time

Somewhere along the way I must've gotten so lost in the music
that I lost myself right along with it

You had become my Psalms while I was only the beginning of
a melody you couldn't seem to finish

Forever stuck in your loop

Relieve me from the confusing nature of your heart's verse
Repeating the same chorus of wanting then having then leaving
and
wanting then having then disappointing
      Baby,
      take
      me to
the bridge

Cause I need my requited love
One that will call and respond
Give and take
A harmonious tune
A 174 hertz healing tone
A *"driftin on a memory, ain't no place i'd rather be" love*

Love
                        was
              never
          destined

for you and me

Was it?

Gm7   Abmaj7   Abmaj7/B
ain't____ no place I'd   rath - er be   tha
that touch-es   me when the   morn-ing comes; fee
can't____ feel in - se - cure a - gain. You
lov - ing   you.
"The Listener" by Emoni Jackson

Entangled Affections

I keep trying to convince myself that it wasn't love because
 love is not painful

Love heals

Unless maybe it was never the act of loving you that ailed
me but the reality that we were not created for one another

I don't want to believe that, however it seems to be true
and knowing this while still loving you is what ails me

So maybe this is love

Just not one we are able to keep

I Think We Need Space

I can feel the hesitation in your spirit
The reluctance in your being
The rebellion of it all in your eyes
as your spine shifts, stretching itself to form a hug

Even your body rejects the changes we endure
Yet,

You

do

not

say

a word

The Letting Go

Today I let you go in the choice to not scroll through
and see who you have found to replace me

Today I let you go in how I stopped comparing myself to
who you want and what I'm not

Today I let you go in realizing that I traded one addiction
for another
swapped my depression for you
called it love
chased the rare highs
endured the constant lows
found comfort in the chaos

Today I let you go in the realization that I loved you
but you never loved me back

Today I let you go in staying in, sacrificing my desire
to be with friends to protect myself from your flirtatious eyes

Today I let you go in the obsessing over someone new
just to admit to myself that no one compares to you

Today I let you go by asking for space

Today I texted you anyway

Today I will forgive myself for not being so good at walking away

Today I let you go in the authenticity of acceptance

Today I let you go in your confessions of loving men
more than you could ever love a woman

Today I let you go in the rupture those words sent
through my eager-for-you heart

Today the letting did not go
Today I held on

Today I chose to hold on to each fantasy, each day dream
of you and me

Today I let you go when I said I loved you and you
could not say it back

Tomorrow I will repeat this ritual
until the letting has gone and fulfilled its purpose

For today is the last time I will allow you to
break my heart

Today I let you go in the stride of my steps as

I
  Move
    On

Goodbye

Letting you go is difficult
Letting you stay is detrimental

This time I choose myself

Journal Prompts For Letting Go

1. What/who am I holding onto that I need to let go of?
    What attachments or expectations do I have regarding
    this person, situation, or aspect of my life? Are there
    underlying beliefs or past experiences that contribute
    to these attachments or expectations?

2. How is holding on to this person, situation, or aspect
    of my life affecting me and those around me?

3. What boundaries do I need to establish to protect my
    emotional well-being in this process of letting go?

4. What vision do I have for my life once I've let go of
    what no longer serves me? How can I align my actions
    and intentions with this vision as I move forward?

5. What self-care practices can support me in healing as
    I navigate the process of letting go?

Affirmations For Letting Go

1. I release what no longer serves me with love and gratitude

2. I let go of fantasies and illusions, and embrace reality with clarity and acceptance

3. I release attachments and create space for growth and transformation

4. I forgive myself and others for any pain or hurt caused, and I release it with compassion

5. I let go of fear and embrace the unknown with courage and curiosity

6. I receive the blessings that come from letting go and moving forward

7. I acknowledge letting go isn't always easy, and I give myself permission to move at my own pace

8. I will go,
    a. Where I am valued
    b. Where I am heard
    c. Where I am loved
    d. Where I am cared for
    e. Where I am considered
    f. Where there is reciprocation

9. I acknowledge that I am worthy and inherently deserving of all these things in any and every relationship I choose to keep in my life

10. I can do hard things

Venture Two
Journeying to Love

Chapter Three
The Book of Love

Brewing

Dressed in iron damask
The tea kettle hums
Takes in a deep breath
and whispers screeching hymns

I prayed for you today

Shea-butter-soft hands and childlike knees
Stories stored in each scar and scrape
Called out to God for you today

*"Dear Heavenly Father, though I do not know who
or where they are, I pray for their protection. I pray
that they find their way to me, in your timing Lord.
I pray that you continue to mold and shape us both
into who you called us to be. Lord, I pray that they
are prepared for me."*

I relieve the singing kettle from the fire on the gas
stove tucked in the corner of my tiny kitchen
I wait keenly as it sits

Fresh out the pot
Sweltering
Dangerous to the touch
We have to be careful here
For if we fall into each other too soon we are
sure to scorch
They say falling is for fools
So imagine you are still cooling
Careful not to burn me

I prayed for you today

Taking the time to strain the ungodly parts so that you
don't choke on me
Steeping these bones so that it is safe for you to sip

I don't know you yet but I already love you
My thoughts sweat for you

Run in circles for you
Scuttle shin splints barefoot through sharded glass
Bleed for you

Are you tall? An air or fire sign?
Are you Black?
Lord please let them be Black

I imagine you as a tea kettle
Singing above my fire
Each note parallel to each beat my heart hums
Pour into me love
Let's settle into each other here
Ripen here
Engross ourselves in the honey and suckle sweetness
of stability
We are safe here

I prayed for us today

At times my Gemini fiddles my moods
And my Leo overpowers my strut
I receive lack of attention as a reason to cause feuds
When I get excited my mouth will refuse to shut

Some days I am tea and others tequila
Most days I am both
Yet somehow I still feel your yearning for me

Dressed in iron damask
The tea kettle takes in a deep breath
And belts out the kind of notes that glass shatters to
Singing prayers of healing
Prayers of patience
The kind God speaks of
Singing all along

"I am ready for love"

Song of Solomon

Am I on the edge of each of your thoughts

Do you choke or chew my name back down to what
could have been

Am I still myself in each of your day dreams

Did you know of soulmates before our spirits chose
one another

Does your heart beat faster from the glance of my eyes

At First Sight

It was last year on a Tuesday
When the wild lilacs embarked on the journey of bowing
at the soil that stretches
To lifting their eyes in adoration towards God,
rendering reverence for early April bloomings

Like the lilac

My roots settled into your soil
And my prayers have been wrapped in you ever since

Smog

I have tried to stop loving you

                                 I have failed a thousand times

I was fearful of the purity of your breath
the air your care transmitted
I have not known such a great thing before
It is in the depths of your gaze where I lose all
understanding of such fear

Before you I only knew of pollution and called it love
Before you I only knew of charcoal lungs, congested
coughs and called it home
Before you I only knew thick fog of toxicity and called
it affection
Choked by the fumes of false promises
Previous flings and unrequited yearnings
Ripping rifts through my heart's ozone
But you are like a breath of fresh air
Healing
Hope in the threat of environmental decay

My asthma flares up when you're away
My throat shrinks in rebellion
My lungs go on strike and picket for your return

You lighten my air

Our love continues to grow into a force of nature,
Able to rebuild itself
Able to withstand the global warming of
past heartache and future trials

I can breathe again

with you

The Night Belongs To Us

In the interim of dusk and dawn
I find myself lost in the linger of your leftover loving
Body bent at the hood of your altar
I stir spellbinding sermons
Lining my fingers at the pit of your beginning
Conjuring our consecrating ceremonies to a
blue-noted end
I marvel at what sorcery you secrete
What splendor we source
Tracing eyes along the breaking of caramel skin by
sienna stretch marks
The story they tell hypnotize me into otherworldly delirium

Hands, clammy and soft, sort at the round of your breast
scavenging for whatever trash I can treasure
I am okay here
With the scraps of you
The unwanted parts
The deemed "undesirable" scars of past lovers
The secret sunsets you shadow

In the greeting of sun I am left clenching the scent
of your shirt
With the magic of last night cluttering my mind
Reciting nocturnal invocations
Praying for the showing of stars
More of your time

   Always needing a taste of your affection

In the interim of dusk and dawn
Pack mutates to lone
Here I become your night thing
Wandering wolf
Your crescent moon, stardust, black-footed fling
Last night we made love like the sun would
no longer rise
Like heartbreak is a distant cousin who only comes
around on occasion

   Always needing a dollar

I bow to the rough howl pleading into my void
Wet-nosed cravings digging at my holy ground
I share my sacred parts here
Soft and soaked soil to bury your bones
Arms spread like harvest sod

Always needing another to hold

In the interim of dusk and dawn
I give in to your hunting incantations
wolf-like hunger and sorceress tales declaring that
the night belongs to us
In this short period of time you are mine
Here we turn rummaged goods into gold
Recycled bits made whole from wind-like breath
gusting off the tip of shooting star wishes
In the stillness of night our bodies cruise alongside
the constellations in one another
Shifting of the tides
Here I become your hare moon

Always needing your love

Springtime Bulbs

Just as the sun hugs March daffodils
How they rise in reciprocal reach

You and I were drawn together
out of a need
for loving

Cuttin Teeth

This feels like teethin all over again
Tha newness
Tha growin pains
Tha sweet reward
Thrustin through thick gums like milk is goin
outta style
Like applesauce and Similac just don't feed me
tha same
Coral pink and pigmented purple
accompanied by blood besmeared

Lips like mom's shushin prayers
Arms rockin me so warm that my fever flees in
search of frost
Tongues like ice soothin tha growin pains
Patient eyes enthralled as crooked teeth emerge

I am learnin to chew all over again
Swollen tenderness rippin through ripe peaches,
dad's freshly caught bluegills, and soul food on
a Sunday

Both of your names salivate in my mouth, soft and
easy to swallow
Careful not to cavity my gums
I am prepared to share this meal with you
You are both tongue and cheek
I am jaw
Repeatedly occludin and openin, occludin and openin
Allowin us to nourish one another

I am learnin to love all over again
Flossin out tha spoiled debris
Welcomin affirmin flavors to melt on my tongue
Savorin your dauntless laughs as they dance across papillae

Nervously dippin the tip of tongue in forbidden fruit
savorin tha consumption of unfamiliar things
Tha trinity of us indulge in cravins once feared
Is it safe here?
Safe like hot soup without bein seared?
Like pistachio gelato absent of that sharp bite of sensitivity?

I finally feel ready to chew
I am ready to love all over again
But this time, I want to try it with the two of you

$^2\!/_3$ (Two-Thirds)

Hangover balled up, lodged in my throat
BC powder bitters my tongue
Brunette brown sheets effuse your cologne, her perfume

Flashes of last night occupy my mind
Starved eyes surrender their ache
Fingers grasping
Drawing me in closer

How can I focus when you blanket my day dreams?

I know that she has all of you
And you, all of her
A fear that leaves me displaced
Though moments of just you and me reject this notion
I must wonder if there is space in your heart
for me too
Do we exist in her absence?
Should we exist in such perplexing places?

I have no desire to be a weekend lover
A Sza singer
A fun time, night secret as your fantasy swinger
Prove to me that you want me in the daylight

Reach for me

Holding hands
Swinging arms
Frolickin across pin needles
Skipping to the rhythm of your tongue

Reach for me
For I will not wait here bleeding for you long
Reach for me before I am forced to save myself
Patch and peroxide pricked heels
Wrap my wounds in distance and "nos" until they
go numb
Until I can walk with you again as just a friend

Fleshing out your intentions in between whiskey
pickle backs and cautious ogles
I wait for you to extend

Reach for me
Before these needles pierce too deep and all I have
to live off of is your smile alone
That saccharine smile of yours
What morals I'd forget
Crimes I'd commit
Sins I'd permit
Boundaries I'd erase
Self I'd replace
To morph into your lips
Just to keep that smile on your face

You feel like repentance from Saturday night on a
Sunday morning
In the springtime
A fresh start
Like gravity lost
Cloud hopping in clean air
Dizzily twirling into locked eyes
Spiritual serenades
Intoned over flame orange poppy fields

She has you
And you her
Yet I do not mind,
if there is space for me too
Equally intertwined

Cause love   is

                never   selfish

Muse

Before you, love was limited to the solace found in new
books, blues records, and the sound of rain dancing its
way down my window
But now, they pale in comparison to the passion you spark

When you are away for more than a second, I scratch
and sniff my limbs in hopes of finding you there
I exhale the reminisce of your essence burrowed between
my fingertips and nails
And embrace the leftovers of your presence until
you return

Before you, I never knew the healing power of intimacy
The comfort of swaddling arms enveloping body
Being held by you feels like coming home
Your love transcends all fears of being hurt
In your arms, peace and passion coincide

So let the rain fall, and the books speak,
For in your love, I am home, I am brave
With you, my love, come what may,
For in your love I am safe, I am okay

So let the records spin the blues,
For you are the ink that flows through every word I write
My art
My muse

Love of My Life

I tried to settle as just your friend

It

    Ain't

        Workin

Call Me Sometime

Tell me you miss me
I need you to want me too
God. Let this be love

Ego

You are drinking a beer
Chatting with our friends
about the new Black-owned IPA you've discovered
and the importance of the Black dollar
I step out of the bedroom laced in a long sheer skirt
with a tight corset the color of the moon

You stop mid-conversation
Eyes unblinking
Your woes drown at the sight of me
Then you gasp for lost air and sternly say

"You gotta take that off"

I walk
Slowly
Seductively
Toward your scent
Lure you closer by caressing your beard
And whisper into your ear

"Fuck the patriarchy and the fragility of male ego"

You hear:

"So take it off"

We laugh

You look into my eyes

Suddenly our friends disappear into the shadow
of connection
It is just you and me

Love flushes you, draining your insecurities

Our lips raft along rippling thoughts
Meeting at moat
Exiling castles of pride

Communion

Yesterday you asked me what my intentions are with you

Two months ago I knew you as the woman whose name
had climbed into my limbs and made them its home
The woman who exists so soft and so loud cozied in my thoughts

When I approached you to introduce myself
our eyes met and the coordination fled from my figure
clumsy crowded my tongue, clenched my jaw, strangled my vocal chords
My mouth morphed gay
No longer able to even speak straight
S t u t t e r i n g
Sinuating speech
Then you spoke
        I manage to respond
"Hi my name is TK"

Yesterday you asked me what my intentions are with you

Well for starters I intend to stop gawking and gabbling
long enough to ask you on a date that will never happen

A month ago
My exulting of you did not stop
when your lips revealed themselves as tectonic plates
as the words "I have a partner"
sent seismic waves up my bones and through my chest
This chest of mine in which you live
The fault lines were non existent
Unable to predict the shift occurring
In this chest of mine
in which you live
Anointing the sod, holding infinite intimate possibilities of us
High
       as the night that you asked to kiss me
And we flirted

    And we flirted

      And we flirted until mosquito hours
Full of desire
Full of need
That night that turned into morning
That night when you placed mountains that are too large to
climb in places where flowers should grow
Inhibiting the honey I'd have to offer
That night that turned into mourning
Full of dying "we long tos and we couldn'ts"

I know that my longing for you is futile
Yet my stubborn hands demur the need to excavate
your bones
Arms left limp from efforts to shovel your name out of these limbs
You are still here
Not going anywhere
Existing in the pauses of my wind
The cracks of my landscape
Planting your soft and loud whispers in my garden

Yesterday you asked me what my intentions are with you

Two weeks ago
The D'ussé must have Houdinied your shame because "I want you"s
began to dance from your throat and land on my cheek
Gravitating you so close that my lungs filled with your pheromones
And our hearts began to pray together
Proselytizing our morals to partake in communion

Yesterday you asked me what my intentions are with you

You: So soft and so loud
Me: Your terrain

Next week when we congregate
I will not be as prudent
I will know you as the woman who caused earthquakes in my being
Whose hands fingered through my roots in search of salvation
Whose lips sang hymns of "I lust yous"
To which I will reply
"*Beense* we here, we might as well have church"

Taboo Instincts

Eradicated
morals. By way of Patron
Scripture precludes us

Vain

I love God
and my girlfriend

Is my repentance in vain?

Proverbs

I am told the tongue holds the power of
life and death
so I wrote you into a poem
and spoke you into a prayer
manifesting the emergence of
your soul and mine

When we kissed
for the first time
I found gold laced between my teeth

Found surrender
safe for once
as soft lips traced
ribbons of riches
down copper skin

It is in the sunlight
that rises within your eyes
whenever you see my face

It is in the way you kiss me
as if I am
your good thing

And yes, I know
that I should be writing
about the war on
us queers and
us who depend on school lunches to eat and
us who need free health care to survive and
us who are so dark that
albuterol won't save us when
we "can't breathe"
no inhaler able to remedy the sting
of police kneeling on our necks and
us who are being snatched right out of our homes
and
us whose children are being killed and
us whose homes are being bombed and
us who are born into wars we never asked for and
us who cry and
us who laugh and
us who bleed and
us who love and
us who curse and
us who pray

I am told

the tongue holds the power of life and death

so I wrote you into a poem

and spoke you into a prayer

manifesting a world in which

I can love you without threat

When we kissed for the first time

I touched heaven

It is in the shape of your lips

a pearly gate

promising priceless treasures of eternal love

It is in the way

my strong softens in your presence

It is in the way

I am excited to cook for you

after an eight hour shift

fried chicken, yams, mac and cheese, cabbage, corn bread,

and blueberry buckle for dessert

just because i know how much you love to eat

And yes, I know
that I should be writing
about the war outside our door
but instead I am writing of you
of loving you anyways

And yes, I know
that I should be writing about the war outside
but when I look into your eyes
I am reminded of God
of peace
of a future

And I think to myself
that maybe this poem is resistance
that maybe, just maybe

LOVE IS THE REVOLUTION

Journal Prompts for Romantic Love

1. What are your personal values and beliefs about love and romantic relationships? How have they been shaped by past experiences?

2. Create a list of qualities and traits you need in a partner. Create a list of qualities and traits you want in a partner. Create a separate list of those qualities and traits you are willing/not willing to compromise on. How do these traits complement you? (This prompt is not limited to romantic love but for all relationships in your life: friends, family, etc.)

3. Explore any fears or insecurities you may have related to romantic relationships. How do these emotions influence your approach to love, and how can you work through them?

4. Reflect on a memorable moment of love or connection. What made this experience special, and how can you cultivate more moments of love and connection in your relationships?

5. How would you describe your last romantic relationship in one word?

Affirmations for Romantic Love

1. I trust in the journey of love, knowing that it unfolds with grace and ease

2. My heart is open to receiving the deep and fulfilling love I desire

3. In all of my relationships, I communicate my needs and boundaries with clarity and compassion

4. I deserve love, just as I am in this moment

5. I deserve romance

6. I release desperation and allow myself to attract genuine love

7. I do not settle for minimum effort in my pursuit of finding a loving partner

8. I give and receive intentional effort in romantic relationships

9. I am inherently worthy of love and respect

10. I am grateful for the love that surrounds me and look forward to deepening my connections

Chapter Four:
Book of The Divine

"I find I am constantly being encouraged
to pluck out some one aspect of myself
and present this as the meaningful whole,
eclipsing or denying the other parts of self.**"**

– Audre Lorde, *Sister Outsider: Essays and Speeches*

Wonderfully Made

I am Black, I am woman, I am queer, and I'm loved by God.

Belonging in the Margins

A lot of people have an issue with me being queer
People that I love
Though they refuse to admit it
They show me through passive jokes and
indirect comments
They refuse to admit to themselves out of fear of
being homophobic

They will never unlearn this absence of love until they
acknowledge it as so

I've never felt like an abomination until humans told me
I chose this gayness
This humanness
This cherry-picking "love" you give me
Loving bits of me but not all of me

A lot of people have an issue with me being queer
People that I love
And they have no problem voicing it
They show me through direct comments
Through promises of missing my wedding, if I were to
ever have one

Through drunken tequila-tainted lips
Through tattooed skin covered in mixed linen
with judgment sitting confidently in their chest
I've never felt like an abomination until humans told me
I chose this gayness
This oppression
This constant fighting
Having to prove my worthiness of God's love

For the first time, I am not proud of who I am
For the first time, I question God for not sending me
a man to love
For not making me in ways in which I could love that
man the way I love Renee

For the first time, I do not feel loved amongst the congregation
I am not loved by them as God loves me
I am made less human for "sins" I did not choose for myself,
unlike my sin of drunkenness and yours of lust and linen
I am made shameful here, by another human, a fellow Christian

For the first time, love does not cover a multitude of "sins"
You see,
A lot of people have an issue with me being queer
A lot of people that I love

They will never unlearn this absence of love until they
acknowledge it as so

It is days like this that I am reminded of how hard it is
being queer, Christian, and alive

Incessantly

I can feel it knocking at my chest
Snaking its way upward
Hastily hovering above my tongue
Burdens laid at the foot of my chin
Rounding vowels
Shaping sound
Gargling prayers

I tried to swallow love once

Burying godliness inside of my esophagus
Tightening my teeth, tearing at the seams of each trial
Leaky gums
Locked joints
Drooling jaws
Accustomed to stuffing worldly solutions in the spaces of my lips
like broken-down bolus
Drink away my tribulations
Fatten my liver
Leaving me with tummy aches and silver-toothed tales

I tried to swallow love
a few times

Put so much faith in this world
In so-called "friends and family"
In myself

I was left afraid and alone
I began to incessantly call out to you
In those humbling moments the word love became harder to chew
"Fortify me Oh Lord
with the strength you've given David
Shift these ribs
pave passage past the burrow of my belly
through the corridors of my soul
and make me over
Show me who you are"

The bread of life
satisfying every hunger pang
The rosemary seeded in my garden
The peppery herb that sages my stew
The fresh scent of mint in my tea
easing my anxiety
The seeped oil of extra virgin olives
laid at my doorstep

                I tried to swallow love once

Now it lounges in my mouth so comfortably
that I speak of it
As a profession of faith,
I speak of you

My God
My Saving Grace
My One True Love

# Thursdays on Skid Row

Don't need no socks
Don't need no shoes
Jus gimme a hot plate
and play them blues

I do my dance
I skip real high
I sing my song
Yeah, baby I ain't shy

Don't need no man
Don't need no drug
Jus gimme a soft smile
and a hard hug

I clap my hands
I play my tune
I feel this joy
Like winter turned to June

Don't need no priest
Don't need no crowd
Jus gimme a prayer
and a sad cloud

Let tha rain fall fresh upon my flesh and baptize my soul
This is love
My pants may be faded and not without a hole
But I look good when God's grace is glistenin off my skin
This is love baby
Yeah,
"This is what makes me feel human again"

Divine

Last year I saw you in the text of a close friend breaking my heart
I stood there angry and confused
as to why you continue to allow me to be hurt by those
I love
I am now grateful for this release
$$\text{I find you where spirit shifts and the wind sifts}$$
$$\text{Thank you for the letting go}$$

Last month I saw you through the numbers on a phone
as a call from my best friend reaffirmed your will
for my life, even when I felt lost
$$\text{I find you between the wondering and the answer}$$
$$\text{In the friends we share and their prayers}$$

Last week I saw you in a letter of acceptance
for a program that I didn't even apply for
after the denial of an opportunity I thought I wanted
$$\text{I find you where the ocean foam kisses}$$
$$\text{The sand that protects young eggs}$$
$$\text{That releases the hatchlings too}$$
$$\text{I find you in the creases of my eyelids,}$$
$$\text{mapping out the path ahead}$$

Yesterday I saw you through the jaundiced yellow eyes
of a copper-toned, salt-and-pepper-bearded man
He stood in between the lanes of a red traffic light
Yesterday I felt your presence when, after slipping him
a few dollars
That seasoned human lowered his cardboard sign and
said "I love you"

> I find you in spaces between the wanting and
> > The needing
> > The giving and the grateful

This morning I found you in my will to keep going
I felt weary, but I did not faint
I felt defeated, but I did not quit
I grew tired, but I endured

> > I find you in the pull of my muscles,
> > stretching me in ways I never thought
> > > I could bend
> > > The source of my strength
> > > Building solid within my core
> > > I find you in back of my knees,
> > > keeping me grounded

> And in the finding of you
> I find me too

Surrenderance

"Girl you gon catch a cold out there in that rain"
I can hear momma's voice echoin in my mind as if I was
still all legs and lip,
what she describes as my eleven-year-ol' self
Can hear her sayin I must've lost my mind
That I done got my hair all wet n she not heatin tha hot
comb up again

But ion care none

I ran in tha rain today
Felt freedom for tha first time
Strides long like tha Nile itself
Chest out
      Chin high
          Clouds gatherin
                        God roarin
Blessin each splash peckin at my ankles

Glasses opaque n speckled wit drops

When I could no longer see

n my limbs began to pout from exhaustion

I found it easier to just   surrender

To let spirit n wind guide my steps rather than runnin

against it

I felt safe in tha middle of tha storm

I felt free

The Unearthing of Me

I am tree
of soil
of leaf
of bark
stunted in the stench of salted sod
What jaded jones jammed in my joints
congesting my bones is this?
What demonic contortions have I been bending to
the will of the world
shapes I have never seen
What pest-like sin attacking my leaves
singeing soil sitting beneath bark

In the destruction of it all
During the wreckage
After the burning
Through the thickest of fog, blinding my sight
Like David, I will trust your guidance oh Lord

I am tree
of root
of branch
of life itself
held captive under the heavy cement of sidewalk
How desperately I want to know the breath of life
beyond these stunted stems
Breaking branches, reshaping to find such air
I am here
suffocating in the sink of sidewalk caulked pathways

I know not why the thwarting has come but I will trust you
oh Lord
I will praise you with every ring marking the passage of time
Your word shall be pith of my trunk
crackling cemented relationships, breaking and buckling
them above my roots
I watch as friends tiptoe over the sinus pinching screams
of my brokenness
I call out to you

It is here where I do not die
It is here that I do not fall

I feel the dance of your fingers pruning out the dead
wood and infected leaves

You are the god of recovery

I feel the heaven in your hands plowing at my being
reshaping me from once singed soil
now nutrient rich
fertilizing my growth
I will rise from the ashes as David
against the Amalekites

You are the god of provision

I can feel the furrowing of your will
allowing water to flow
Falling out of fear and into faith
I am tree
planted by the streams of water
I yield fruit in the seasons and my leaf does not wither

I am tree
proceeding with your promise
singing your praises through the dance of my branches
worshiping your name in release of air
from each lending leaf
proceeding with your promise
singing your praises through the dance of my branches

Noise

I wonder what it feels like to experience pure silence
No titter tatter of heels down Figueroa soliciting the temples
they hold up

The rustle of ravens picking palm trees cease to exist
Vagrant voices no longer praying for Christians
to be Christian

Blithe and brim belly roars gifted to us from a neighbor's joke
now hushed

What chaotic peace it must be to live in stillness
I long for the solitude of it all

Just

Me

God

And this silence

I Met Tha Boogeyman at 1612 Francis St.

Once upon a still sky when dawn kissed noon
as the trees stood crooked and spring mayapples umbrella the
chipped sidewalk
ornate with chalk

A young girl wandered frantically across the sidewalk art
with tears in her heart
that crawled their way up her sockets
past her cheek and down her chest
dragging fear behind them
washing away the chalk

Unaware of the eyes nearby that stalk

Banging on the neighbors door
No answer, no soul to implore
Another house or two down from her vacant home
She knocked
and was yet again left alone

Crouching down on her knees
Praying someone could hear her abandoned pleas

A sound emerges from behind
hope straightened her back
desperate for respite
Faith slowly lifted her chin and
Shock stretched her eyes

Boysenberry black stick-like forelimbs joined to long stilt
slacks hovered above her
molesting the clouds
Silence swallowed her cries in one breath
A gawking grimace hollow shape of a man
reaches down
snatching the child

A forlorn fiendish fright

His harsh, husky hushhhhhhhes hissed my ear
The knob of the door ahead begins to hymn
"you betta run

       betta run

           betta run

               oh you betta run

                       run

                           run

you betta run to tha city of refuge"
as its hinges clapped and the wood rails foot slapped to
the spiritual
emerged from the other side a woman who keeps the sweetness
of orange Creamsicles and Choco Tacos fresh on my tongue

Screaming is tucked away behind my left lung
too fearful to tiptoe its way up my throat
My small body hit the stairs slope
Thrown to the concrete that chips
Breath fled my body through my lips

The shape in all its baleful, baneful, brutishness
briskly becomes shadow

The ice cream lady rapidly removed me from the
concrete to her home
I sat on this woman's plastic-protected couch
waiting for my breath to find its way back into my flesh

I began to bleed

I was covered by the blood
Hallelujah

"Francis Street" by Takayla P. Carlton

I Met God During a Ten-Minute Breath Work Exercise

I lay flat, back to mat
taking in a deep breath for 4

. . . , 3, 2, 1

Hold for 4

. . . , 3, 2, 1

Release for 4

. . . , 3, 2, 1

Repeat

Your Spirit
rings through me like evening bells calling believers
to worship
Cells hum to the tune of your presence like the vibration
of mallet to singing bowl, casting out all anxieties
The Holy Spirit is present here
within me
speaking peace
speaking stillness

Eyelids slowly peek past palm leaves
Clouds move to make way for new beginnings
The sun hugs every part of me
It is God

reassuring me that everything will be alright

In this moment
I am loved

Meditation

Hands starfish-stretched in front
Heels planted in the soil
Head hung loose
Hips thrusting toward the sky
A long deep breath in
A vocal exhale out

I can feel you in the stretch of my back
In the release of pain through each exiling exhale
In the healing that comes with each new breath
I feel your presence in the present
keeping me grounded

This is my favorite type of prayer, in meditation with you

I feel you in the peak of the sun
In the distant honk and siren screams
In the rumbling of the helicopter above, churning
through
the clouds

I feel you in the dance of the branches
in the rustling of leaves
in the twisting of the wind snaking its way up my legs,
reminding me that I am still here
Through the low-pitched grunts of koi fish
discussing this morning's heron sighting

This is my favorite type of love, in communion with you

Sound bowl songs and singing birds bring me
back to myself
back to you
                    The source of my solace

This is where I feel most loved

Ode To tha Men Who Raised Me

Top turned

Scarlet seats

Rollin rims

Fannin fros

Vivacious views

Diamond in the back sunroof top diggin the scene

with a gangsta lean oooos

Father daughter car rides sunshine me

like buyin a used record with its faint scratches and

all its history

Sunshine me like pistachio gelato coolin my tongue

on a Milan summer afternoon

Car rides with you have always been a boon

You showed me classic music in classic cars

Rear view and side mirrors ideal

Seat leaned low

One hand on tha wheel

And most importantly, Gucci Mane on tha stereo

You taught me how to drive

Screamin Sirens
Tiltin turns
Wreckin windows
Shatterin shards
Police came a swarmin
Mamma came a stumpin
Hearts went a jumpin

And they let us go

You took me on my first high speed chase

Sharin
Sisterly secrets
Sisterly seein
Sunken sternum
Sustained sobbin
Shrouded schoolin
Studyin stares
Brokenhearted Brittany
Repeat after me "I Takayla Passionelle am beautiful,
I Takayla Passionelle am worthy, I Takayla Passionelle
will not tolerate disrespect, I Takayla Passionelle will
neva be "Brittany-ed"

You taught me to never let anyone play with my heart
poured into me confidence

Sat with me on creaky wooden steps at 1606 Francis Street
and showed me how to tie my laces
Sprinted me down Crofton in cul-de-sac races
Hopscotched in our flip flops down F block past street light
o'clock so we got popped by momma with ha fingas locked

That stung almost as much as when you
Started drinkin ice cold wata, went from servin dogs to
eatin wit em
I thank God you went to jail instead of hell cause you got
clean behind that cell
When you stole from me I had to swallow tha pill
Neva turned my back on my brotha n neva will

You showed me how to forgive

Swallowin smoke
Beepin buzzers
Wispin rags
Damn Kayla how you burn Ramen
The stove is better but tha microwave's common
Open the package with steady control
Place the noodles in a bowl
Pour seasonin as it bubbles hotter
Shit, I forgot to tell you to add water

You taught me how to almost burn the house down

When the sweat of your brow led me to a school where
I had to pronounce my e's and r's when I spoke
Out in Avon with all tha white folk
Where they sprayed "nigga" on our family construction
site and we was ready to fight—
But you didn't have any hate to spread so we sat and
prayed for them instead
Kinda like how I pray for you

You showed me what it means to give grace

When stroke struck momma
I watched you bath her, dress her, and feed her as well

You displayed the meanin of "through thick and thin,
in sickness and in health"
Thank you for that

"My name is KK and I'm here to say. I'm six years old and I always pray"

You taught me how to rap
When tha corner store off Madison sold me stale
Hot Crunchy Kurls
you showed me how to get my money back

See, I was raised by gangstas and saints unda tha same roof
so I will pray for you but could neva be prey for you

You taught me how to stand up for myself

And I know they only see you as gangstas and thugs
As targets and game
As animals with Godly expectations
As cheat sheets for fashion, music, and fame
But in my eyes you'll always be the prototype that God made
for other fathers to emulate
In my eyes you are the embodiment of love
In my eyes you are a god though they label you "inmate"
In my eyes you are Sunday school lessons, Curtis Mayfield
car rides, prayin hands, protectin palms, our sacred sacrifice
from above
Though they've tried to diminish you to a white man's primage
In my eyes you are brother, uncle, Papa, and Pops

    You are the ultimate creator in his own image

Religious
After Mike The Poet

My style is communion crackers and grape juice every first Sunday

My style is late night poetry sessions after an early mornin Monday

My style is hip hop in drop tops to rock rock to the Planet Rock,
don't stop

My style is Sanford and Son Saturdays with Dad laughin at Red Fox
and his junk shop

My style is velvet kisses and mournsome goodbyes

My style is a lot of brown sugar and a little vanilla in grandma's sweet
potato pies

My style is givin like three wise men prayin for a savior

My style is "wreckless" like an Alicia Keys love on my worst behavior

My style is period, you did that, and okay I see you young blood
feather fluffin

My style is back talkin back smackin humblin

My style is choosin you

My style is choosin you though you don't chose me too

My style is choosin me

My style is choosin me finally choosing reciprocity

My style is forgiveness

My style is repentance

My

       style

             is

Religious

Divine Solace

Like hot water and tea tree oil cleansin
my mosquito bites

Your presence soothes me

Journal Prompts for Divine Love

1. Reflect on the qualities of love that you associate with God or your spiritual beliefs. How do these qualities manifest in your interactions with others?

2. Have there been times when you've struggled to believe in or feel connected to Divine Love? What factors influenced these struggles, and how did you navigate them?

3. Reflect on a moment when you felt deeply connected to a sense of Divine Love or presence. Describe the experience and how it impacted you.

4. Consider how your relationship with the Divine shapes your capacity to love and forgive.

5. Write a letter to God expressing your thoughts, feelings, and questions about love.

Affirmations for Divine Love

1. I surrender to the Divine Love that heals all wounds and restores me to wholeness

2. I seek to love others as the Divine loves me, with patience, kindness, and selflessness

3. I am fearfully and wonderfully made

4. I am guided and supported by Divine Love in every moment

5. God's love for me is infinite and unwavering

6. I am a vessel of God's love, sharing His compassion and grace with those around me

7. I am open to God's guidance and direction in my relationships, trusting Him to lead me towards His perfect will

8. I am worthy of God's love just as I am

9. God's love casts out all fear, allowing me to love boldly and without reservation

10. The love and wisdom of the Divine accompany me throughout my secular sojourn on this earth, illuminating my journey with grace and clarity

Chapter 5

The Book of Self

Praise Prose

For so long I thought of ways to "better" myself
to your liking
So that you would love me more

      Now I only desire to better myself in efforts
            to love God more
         to love the God that is within me
              that is me
          and that lives through me

Black Body Blessin

If I am ever blessed enough to meet a Black woman
I would be reminded

of favor
of holy
of miracle

If I am ever called upon to love a Black woman
her stretch marks would not know of shame
but of reverence

for
the bending she's done
the sanctuary she's been
the rivers she's carried

If I am ever blessed enough to meet a Black woman
I'd speak in tongues just to thank her in her native
speech
plant seeds of praise into the fullness of her
and watch as she sprouts out
centuries of

a nation
a culture
a reason

If I am ever called upon to love a Black woman
            her scars would not know of pain
                but of glory

                                                for
                                    the crosses she's carried
                                    the sacrifices she's been
                                    the wars she's conquered

        I'd paint her cellulite as a hundred scattered stars, a map
                            placed there by a God himself
                            so that we may know of freedom

If I am ever called upon to love a Black woman
            when she wraps me in her arms
                I'd hold her back
                                        squeeze her long
                            compress my condolences into her soul
                        let my tears run rivers down her back
            cleansing her from the mockery her body has known
                                    the imitation it's been

    I would stream brown escape from a red cup
        in memorial to the all the pieces she's lost

                    sink a requiem into the soil
                         storing stolen bones
                    scattered across foreign land

I would rejoice in the existence of wide hips
                    spanned thighs
                    sagging breast
                              kneel at her feet
                         anoint them with oil
                         witness her divine
                         and call her good
                         call her beginning

If I am ever blessed enough to love a Black woman

I know I will have loved the closest thing to God

Exfoliating

I am shedding my skin
Performing all of the self-care tips that my *Instagram* feed suggested

I am attached to the dead cells and proteins that once kept my body
protected

My therapist, a Black woman, told me that I don't have to be strong
all the time
I did not believe it
I'm not even sure if she did

Black woman,
the title "strong" to you is like carbon dioxide to a plant
It makes you grow more vigorously, even in closed environments,
and encourages you to thicken your leaves
However, too much carbon dioxide kills the plant

I am attached to the many grooves and patterns pieced perfectly
together making mazes that rough hands once caressed in search
of loving me

You have no choice but to be strong when you bear the burden
of burying broken bones that were once Black boys: your son's,
your nephew's, your father's, your lover's, your brother's bloody
bare bodies

Black woman,
you are tired of being glorified for being strong cause yo mamma
aint raise no fool so you are wise enough to know that the presence
of strength equates to the presence of heartache and who will help
you when you break?

Though I perform these transformative remedies of self-care, I am
still attached to the tough tissue, hair follicles, and sweat glands
that have many times saved my life

Black woman,
you may not invite it in but
the soot of everyone's pain creeps into your crevice, polluting every
corner and cranny of your brain
except your own

You have been raped, ridiculed, thrown in lions' dens with nothing
but a prayer and this skin

Black woman,
your emotions are intrinsic and you deserve to no longer repress
them as a survival skill it's time as Black women we vetoed that bill

Black woman
you have birthed and built the beings of this world,
reigned on
thrones, led revolutions, freed slaves, spit spirited gospels
of love
through speech and song

Black woman,
it is in your blood to be strong

At times being Black, and woman, and alive is exhausting
but you keep going

Black Woman,
       You   deserve   to   heal
     so as the layers of your skin continue to peel

             Let It

A Journey of Self-Reflection

I met a ~~girl~~ woman last night

I called off work today

We did unspeakable things in the bathroom

My manager reminded me
why I should quit

I broke a promise I made to God last night

I decided to sit in the sun
and rest today

I broke a promise I made to myself last night

My mind doesn't know
stillness today

We are both disappointed in me

Today I did not think of you
obsessively

I met a ~~girl~~ woman last night

I drunk emailed my therapist at 2:00am

Today I did not think of my
shortcomings as failures

Syd and I made the uber driver
laugh on the way home

Today I pinned my dirty laundry
to the clotheslines within
my journal pages

I began to sort the fitting from the too-small and outworn

This feels a lot like love

I have a lot of packing to do

I have a lot of unpacking to do

I pray for the patience to get it done

Unrequited

The puttying of you came first
Tugging and tucking toes to fit into their likeness
Reshaping yourself
less body and more caulk-like
Cracked bones and holes to fill
You,
            now bent being

                            How did you end up here?
                                            You, so bold and confident
                                            You, so exuding of love
                                            You, so giving
                                            You, so wise
                                            You, so beautiful
                                            Dark skin and thick thighs
Nestling yourself in the warmth of their whispers
Sketching your self-portraits down the stretch of their back
Exhaling formless lips, ushering your humble kisses to their
quickly departed feet
Finding yourself folded into a contorted love

                            How did you end up here?
                                            You, so worthy
                                            You, so divine
                                            You, so God
                                            You, so free spirit, heavenly fine

You are the shit

How dare they not love you back?

Love you properly

Love you pretty and bolded like size twenty italicized text

Love you so loud it bursts outside the one inch margins

Love you beyond fear

Love you consistently

Love you without confusion

How couldn't they

              Love

                  You?

                                You, so poetry

                                You, so muse

                                You, so spark

                                You, so fire

                                You, so fuse

You are the shit?

And shouldn't tolerate anyone who doesn't see

or can't handle it

In all of the slipping in and out of yourself
Did you ever wonder
If they even found
You
Worthy
Of the love you so
Heedlessly give?
And why oh why do you keep breaking
Yourself for unrequited love?

I know it is hard for you to let go, so I will hold your hand
as you walk away
I will yell your worthiness until you are no longer
deaf from longing
god, you are such a goddess
Worthy of worship
Meant to love and be loved in return

I know that you pour into others so fearlessly, so I will be
sure to pour into you until you no longer ask
"Why don't they love me the same, or back, or at all?"

Baby girl,
don't you know you the shit,

You so compassionate

You so graceful in every view

You so spiritually attuned

You so radiant in all you do

You so natural hair and pretty white teeth

Slim waist and a large

ass-

pirant

personality

How did you end up here?
Staying in places where you have to beg for love
Where choosing you is hard to do
Like you ain't that bitch
Been that bitch, and will always be that bitch

You gather your poetry, that porcelain smile, those caulk-crusted
bones, and baby

Love

On

You

This time

And Love On Me

I think I'll stay in tonight
I think I'll let my body rest and spirit mourn

I think I'll stay in tonight
I think I'll sit and think of all the ways I tried to teach
you how to love me
Ways I thought you should

I should have just met you where you were
Maybe then I would have not been so disappointed

I think I'll stay in tonight
I think I'll forgive you for loving me
the best you could
I think I'll stay in tonight and forgive me too
for putting those expectations on you

Continuously choosing to love someone who could not
love me in the ways that I needed to be loved,
was self-sabotage
no matter if they intended to or not

I think I'll stay in tonight
Spend some time alone
Extend myself grace
for loving you so hard and not moving on so easily

I think I'll stay in tonight
I think I'll purge my spirit of all of my minds
unfeeling expectations

I'm going to stay in tonight
And
  Love
    On
      Me

Gentrified

I was almost gentrified

Gentrified like movin from tha hood
to tha suburbs
at a young age
bilingual like Grand Rapids and tha west side of Chicago at home
but *Avon, Indiana* at school
Gentrified like you got it good we got you
out tha hood
just make sure you leave your AAVE at home n pack yo proper for lunch
so you not misunderstood

Gentrified like my avocado toast needs a little bit of seasoning on it
Like being taught that my Black Panther grandparents were the
real terrorists
Gentrified like "whiter school, better education"

I was almost gentrified

Gentrified like Yessica and Tanisha were my best friends on the playground
Like Black and Brown princesses in my colorin book
But now I'm tha only Black girl in tha class
Only one on tha basketball team that look like me
Only "white girl" in tha family tree

But I'm Black

Black like

Zach from Noodles & Company *in Plainfield, Indiana calling you a coon*

because he is gay

Though white and male

He's still a minority so it's okay

And it's somethin "[his] Black friends let [him] say"

Or Will with his white mother and Black father

calling you "Harriet Tubman" as you sweep the floor and all the others

chuckle in a shameless roar

How he tells you to invite your friends over

because he's never slept with a Black girl before

I'm Black

Black like the fetishization of my body

be blessin

be beneficial

be barbarically beautiful

be blushin compliments

Black like *"Dude it's just a word and all the rappers say it"* Connor says

slurpin in the n word

swooshin and savorin it in between pink gums n

slickly slippin it back out of his lips like

buttered noodles on yo lunch break

I'm Black like sittin in tha same college classroom as my white peers
but walkin in a completely different world
Black like Brown v. Board of Education was supposed to catalyze integration
Black like Mr. Bob makin you sit in tha back of the bus for bein tha only Black
on tha bus
Black like I can't wait to tell Yessica and Tanisha how at school today I learned
about segregation

Black like midnight's hue, rhythm & blues, booty cornbread grew, style sick
like flu
Black like straight-A student, school ambassador, track team captain, student
of the month, and the only Black one too
Black like I got somethin to prove

I'm Black
Black like he doesn't date women who look like me
but "I'm special because I code switch very well"
and when I'm racially abused I never yell
                                        Is it because my accent goes in and out?
Or that my voice was stolen from me so I can no longer shout?

I was almost gentrified
Gentrified like "You don't act like other Black girls. I'm blacker than you"
Black like it's a blessing for you that I'm saved
Cause I try my best to behave
Behave
But doesn't that still kinda make me yo slave?

Gentrified like they start with the laundry mats
and replace them with yoga studios
Gentrified like no more mom and pop shops
that's where the overpriced coffee goes

Gentrified like Mrs. Loretta stayed here for 47 years
Mrs. Loretta gotta wash her clothes too
Got no car but got ills and aches like you
Got no more pharmacy off 3rd to walk to
cause that's where the luxury vet hospital grew

Y'all, I was almost gentrified
Gentrified like Harlem, Boerum Hill Brooklyn,
Lincoln Park, and the United States too

I'm Black like my ancestors wasn't no slaves
but doctors, architects, royalty, and linguists
who created the alphabet
which was stolen from our caves

Gentrified like break the community don't build it
Like segregation no integration
Relocation no accommodation
Incarceration no emancipation

We need

Compensation and reparations
Unification no discrimination

I am Black like the source of love, casting out all of
the oppressions and self-hate you reduced me to
Black like you mutilated us
Yet we still have no hate in our hearts for you
Black like grace
Like the son of God
Who you call Savior

I am love

Love
Love like it's the only thing that can heal
a way of thinking
Love like it's the only way to rebuild a community

I am love

I

      AM

            LOVE

Journal Prompts for Self Love

1. Reflect on your relationship with yourself. What are some areas where you demonstrate self-love?

2. Explore your self-worth and self-esteem. How do you perceive yourself? Do you believe you deserve healthy, reciprocal love and respect? Why or why not?

3. Identify any negative self-talk or limiting beliefs you hold about yourself. How do these thoughts impact your self-esteem, and what steps can you take to challenge and overcome them?

4. Identify one self-care practice that makes you feel loved and cared for. How can you incorporate this practice into your daily routine?

5. Think about a boundary you need to set in order to prioritize your own well-being and self-love. How can you communicate this boundary assertively?

Affirmations for Self Love

1. I am deserving of love and kindness, starting with myself

2. I treat myself with compassion and understanding, even in moments of struggle

3. I prioritize self-care and nurturing my mind, body, and soul

4. I radiate love from within and attract positive energy into my life

5. I am a good person and I don't need to prove it to anyone

6. I am enough, just as I am, and I love myself unconditionally

7. I nourish my soul, spirit, and body because I deserve self-care

8. I give myself permission to grow and develop

9. I am patient with myself as I go through this wonderful journey of life

10. My time and energy are valuable

Notes

The poem "Ego" was inspired by Nikki Giovanni's "Seduction"[1]

The style of writing for "The Night Belongs To Us" was inspired
by poet Kiayla Ryann
@kiaylaryann

The art from "The Listener" was created by Emoni Jackson
@emoni.art

---

[1] Giovanni, Nikki. "Seduction." *Love Poems*. HarperCollins Ebooks, 2008.

About the Author

Takayla P. Carlton, poetically known as "TK," discovered the transformative power of poetry as a means of navigating through the depths of mental health. Initially kept private as a form of personal survival, her poetry has evolved into an expression of emotions and gratitude. Venturing into the realm of public sharing in 2023, TK realized that her words were not just for herself but meant to be shared with others. In her poetry, she seamlessly blends the sacred and the secular, often utilizing alliteration and vivid imagery to craft evocative verses. Inspired by her experiences and the diverse communities to which she belongs, TK's work aims to provoke introspection an provide representation, particularly for marginalized voices within the female, queer, and Black communities. Alongside her poetic pursuits, TK finds joy in spending time with her nieces and nephews, running, fishing, and acting. Holding a bachelor's degree in Theatre, she continues to explore the intersection of art, identity, and self-expression through her poetry, hoping to fulfill its divine purpose within her readers.

Other Titles From Mama's Kitchen Press

Just Be Honest by Alexander James

I'm Writing To Tell You by Jaha Zainabu

Sown In Light by Tekira Briscoe

SOME by Camari Carter Hawkins

All Things Can Be True | Todo Puede Ser Cierto
        by Deyanira Contreras

forged in fire, held in love by Nomad the Poet

Shooting Stars At Sky: the poetry of play, Edited by Mike Bonifer

*Sorority of Bereaved Mothers: poems and stories
from Black Women on pregnancy loss and infertility*,
        Edited by Camari Carter Hawkins